# *USED TO WONDER WHY ME?*

*By*

*Lesley Lofton*

Copyrighted Material

Used to wonder why me?
Copyright ©2022 by Lesley Lofton All rights reserved.
Printed in the United States of America
No part of this publication may be reproduced or used without the Author's permission. Bible verses taken from the KJV, NLT, NASB and NIV versions of the Bible.

Printed in the United States of America
ISBN 979-8-9863283-0-0
Published By Travelin' Light Publishing
Travelinlightpublishing@gmail.com

# Table of Contents

| | |
|---|---|
| Dedication | Page 1 |
| Introduction | Page 2 |
| My Childhood | Page 4 |
| Early Adulthood | Page 9 |
| Turning Point | Page 13 |
| Mom Life | Page 16 |
| Walk by Faith | Page 20 |
| Growth | Page 27 |
| Opinions are everywhere, so is Truth | Page 32 |
| Love Covers All | Page 36 |
| My Experiences with Mental Health | Page 40 |
| Most Recent Events | Page 44 |
| The Devil is a Liar | Page 46 |
| Author's Bio | Page 48 |

# **DEDICATION**

First and foremost, I would like to thank God for His provision. My mom and dad for conceiving me and my children for being my greatest inspiration to make something of myself. Also, my sisters for putting up with me my whole life. Especially my oldest sister Alvina who inspired me to go back to school and find myself.

Last but not least, I would like to thank Darrel for believing in me and encouraging me to start my book.

# Introduction

First and foremost; to be clear, no one delivering the word of God is holier than thou. Yes, the Bible says to be perfect for he is perfect, (Mathew 5:48) but, it also says all men have sinned and fall short (Romans 3:23). I think it is more of being guided in life, through our shortcomings with the word as a map. I am passionate about sharing the word of God. I am also seeking and speaking self-improvement while learning self-confidence, overcoming fears, and working on being authentic in every situation.

I want to transform the lives of those God sends. Now I am not a pastor but would consider myself an evangelist. I simply want to share the word which inspired not only me, but many others who exist in the land of the living.

What makes one want to change? It must come from the heart, which is the groundwork of change. Anyone could say they want to change but it is hard to change without truly desiring it for self. Sometimes we want to stay the way we are simply because it was our norm.

There is discomfort in change. However, if there is a true desire for change, one will bear the discomfort in change. Just until the discomfort becomes nonexistent, due to adjusting to the new events that are inspired from the discomforts.

There is so much joy and peace that comes once victory is won over the enemy in your life. It is about pushing through those overwhelming moments.

Psalms 61:2 is a verse to stand on, "Lead me to the rock that is higher than I when my heart is overwhelmed. Rocky roads will come. It is letting Jesus be the driver. Our trust in him is everything, for you, for me and for all after us.

# My Childhood

My name is Lesley Lofton, I am the baby girl of four girls. I was born February 12, 1989, in Beaumont TX. Now, I do not know how things were back when I was born, but I do know we can only do the best we can with what we are given. We cannot blame anyone for how our life is, something I've done for years. I always thought, well if my parents were better, it would have made me better. It would not have, it probably would have made me worse, feeling superior or entitled. We came from poverty, government assistance, handed down clothes, either walking or with a beat-up ride.

I could not see the other side that was available. Only the norm of my every day, which was rags. My mother was in her addiction to crack when I was a child. I cannot remember the exact age. She eventually weaned herself off the heavy drugs and went to smoking weed and drinking Paul Mason. She struggled with her own demons and needed a way to cope from things in her life that disturbs her. Her mom and Dad were deaf mute, and had mental disorders such as depression, bipolar and schizophrenia which passed down to her, then her children.

My father had high blood pressure because he was often angry, which is where I get my anger issues from. He lost his mom when he was 19. I do not believe he knew his dad, so he had his own way of viewing life. Once I started to see the lifestyle of others, I wondered how people could be so happy and have a prosperous lifestyle. The view I saw as a child made me feel small and worthless. I was not taught to stand my grounds for real life events, so I folded. I still struggle with saying what is on my mind around strangers. We did not attend church so; the power of God was not felt in our home. I feel that they believed, but not to the point of breaking the generational curses that were held over them. I cannot blame them for the situation. We can only work with what we are given, and we can only grow in the areas we truly see an issue with. If we see nothing wrong, we will continue in the current situation. That was what they knew, and they tried. I just pray one day their faith will be strengthened to the point where everything that may have tried to hold them back, loses its power.

When my mom and dad split, I was about seven and this was when my world really shook. I loved my daddy. I was a daddy's girl so when he left, I lost it. I often questioned, if he loved me so much how could he leave like that? I would kick and scream to see him. I was a major headache to everyone around me. At home and at school because I wanted my dad. I would be so angry with my mom, not understanding the reality of the situation. She would try to bring me as much as possible, but the truth of the matter was he did not feel like he was adequate to manage taking care of us. But all I wanted was his time, just for him to be there. That's what got the best of me as a child and became angry and rebellious.

I was interested in being an exotic dancer when I got of age. I could remember a teacher asking me what I want to do when I got older, and I told her in front of the class that I wanted to be an exotic dancer, and I was serious. These feelings came from being lost, with no proper guidance. My mom was more on the "I am going to do me" side, so we didn't get many encouraging messages from her. She was battling her own mental illness she never recovered from as a child, (maybe a little). I could remember going to church with my dad's sister (Aunt Jean) when I was about ten, for the first time. I did not understand the significance of it at that time. We were just going to have something to do. I see now, my aunt saw something that made her take the time out and bring us to church, but I am glad she did. That was when I was introduced to God, right when my dad and mom's divorce was final.

When God is revealed, the enemy will go harder to keep us down, especially if we don't understand the truth. My mom was trying, she took custody of my three cousins, on top of the four of us. We had a house with seven girls. Imagine living with us. There was something every day. A story, a fight, a dramatic moment, good times where we were being sneaky jumping out the windows to see boys. Talk about sorority house. When my cousins came to live with us, we were mean kids at least I know I was. I guess I thought that was normal because it was what I was taught. My dad was an as***** when it came to it. And he could only give us what he knew.

Being territorial; I thought if I made them uncomfortable, they would leave. I reflect to see now, we all needed each other. It is hard to show love for others, when what it takes to truly love hasn't been instilled within. When we were kids, my mom used to just give us the scraps, she would not give us an option of things. I am sure most parents did this in my generation, but not to the extent of kids feeling like animals or step kids. We would get little and nothing else, while the adults would get more of the good stuff. I feel like that really plays the role in my adult life because, now I don't know how to make choices. I am always just taking whatever because I was used to being given whatever, so why not settle for less? That is what I was given.

Looking back at how I grew up, makes me realize why I had reason to not have standards. I did not have those encouraging parents who didn't allow me to settle. I started smoking marijuana at eleven years old. I would take my mom's cocktails and smoke them. There were even times I would get enough to share with some of my friends that I hung with by the time I made it to middle school. Middle school was a bit smoother. I was used to my dad being away and learned to live without him. I was only on weed until I met my oldest son's dad. I was 13, he was 17 and at the time we were smoking embalming fluid. It was the environment we were in. Most of the times we are a product of our environment. He didn't make it out without losing his mind. I wanted to do what he was doing but I got caught up. Thank God, he delivered me out, because it could have been me.

I got pregnant the summer of my 8th grade year. After coming back from living with my oldest sister a few months in Kansas City, Missouri. I had my son at 14, a month before my 15th birthday. Sometimes it's hard to push past everything that is meant to tear you down. One thing I'm learning is, you got to roll with the punches. Can't fold because things get rough, those rough moments are there to bring strength. You can't elevate if everything is always easy. During my tough moments I tell myself, "roll with it."

Everyone does not have the same level of strength or faith. But everyone has a heart to open, to let God's power bring them strength, while seeking Him in his word to bring faith.

Prayer for strength is one thing I have always done when I was pregnant with my first child. I remember praying God to be the best mom I can be, He answered.

I did as much as I could as a 14-year-old with a child. My first job was a summer job at the age of 14. I did not know how I was going to make it, but abortion was not an option. My mom put me out because I wanted to be grown. I lived with my son's dad mom for a while, then went back to my mom. I was always rebellious as a teenager. It seemed like I only wanted to gravitate towards the things and people of the streets. I had positive people offering friendship, but I felt as if I was not good enough to hang out with them.

My mom sent me to live with my dad in Pensacola Florida for a while, then I came back. By 16, I got a job at Whataburger while going to school. Imagine being 16 with a child, still in school, catching a bus to and from school to work. That was nothing but the strength of the Lord. I know it was not strength of my own. I remember smoking weed and saying, I would never smoke or do anything else. It is a gateway drug. Well, it was for me. It is a mind thing and in some instances my mind wasn't strong enough to say no. I saw my mom do it, and it was how she coped. So, in my head it was how I was supposed to cope too. The people around us have an influence on what we do.

# Early Adulthood

Me and my child's father broke up when I was 16. I worked, went to school and managed to graduate top of my class by the age of 17. I started going to Richard Milburn, a charter school, which opened a daycare in dedication to me. They had seen how much I was trying. My mom really did not help much, and my sisters had school as well. I was so grateful. I could remember, me and my cousin getting high before school, and we were called to the front office because someone spotted us, and they threatened to kick us out. That was my shift to not get high by the campus anymore.

I liked to party when I was younger. I was living life with the understanding I had. We were in the clubs at 16, drunk and all. I was still getting high as well. I then met a much older guy; I was 16 he was 26. He was a hood dude, just how I liked them. I got my first duplex when I was 18, and he moved with me. I was fresh out of high school entering college. I did a semester and a half at Lamar Institute of Technology. He was more into chilling and getting high. Being around others who were not about advancement sucked the drive out of me, so I quit school. By this time, I was smoking weed, dip, popping Xanax, drinking, and taking X pills. They say you are what you are around. I did not get it until I disconnected from my closest friend. I thought you can help others grow if they see you trying, but that was far from the truth. Just because they see you do it, does not mean they will automatically jump on board. As hard as it is to believe about some of the people we love, some are dead weight to keep you from moving forward. They keep you from elevating and recognizing that there is more in life than what you experience. Once I left him, due to him going to jail, I got wild. I started to really party and get with different guys. Life has a way of taking us through the loops. Without the right guidance we are sure to sway whichever way the world takes us. Without being fully aware I had a drug addiction it was getting worse by the day. I was 21, a college dropout and a single mom trying to figure out which way to go. It seemed the decisions I started to make were getting worse and worse. I do not know if it was the mentality I was in or the people I was around, but I was doing dumb things. (Like) I was a wannabe thug because I talked that life, but I was not trying to do no time.

At the age of 14 before I found out I was pregnant with my oldest I was caught by the police in an abandoned home. The police officer who came was very inconsiderate with how he handled me. I mean yes, I was doing something I had no business. I had run away from home to be with my boyfriend, so we found an abandoned house to sleep in and put all our things in there. The officer called me all kinds of sluts and whores and I snapped a bit and cursed him out, which in turn got me arrested. That was the longest 5 days 4 nights. That was the only time I had been locked up. I told myself I will not go back to a place like that. I was supposed to just stay a couple of nights, but I lied to one of the people there about my mom hitting me (which she wasn't). That lie made me stay another two days. So, I try to walk in a manner to keep my freedom.

I moved to Louisiana for about a month, trying to start over. I liked living in Metairie but was not ready to be on my own. My cousin lived there, but it was just her and her kids. It didn't work so I came back home. This was when I started using powder. Things went downhill from there. I was working for Lamar and met this guy who lived in the same complex I was in. He was younger than me, but we hooked up. He only smoked weed when we met. By him being with me every day he tried the things I was on, which was dip and powder. I must say that he was the youngest I had ever been with however, he was the best. I was 22, he was 18, but he had a good head on his shoulders though. I should not have given up on him, but we live, and we learn.

From the apartment, we moved into a 3-bedroom house. He was very supportive and would even work plant jobs. I feel like I brought him down with my lifestyle. By this time, my oldest was eight years old. I had always been a good mother to my child however, the drugs held me back from being greater than I was. When him and I broke up, I really went low. I think the things I did to him came back to haunt me. I started seeing more guys and getting even more high. I was the type of chick who only chilled with you if we were getting high.

My old friend was on back page by this time. If you are not familiar with this site it is an escort site. I needed a way to pay for bills and she made an interesting comment. She said, "You are screwing these guys for nothing, why not get paid to do what you like?' At first, I didn't do it until I had to move again, and things really got tight. That's when I finally made the decision. Now, I was on drugs and posting on back page. This was the lowest point of my life. It was 2014, and I was 25. My dad stayed with me for a while. He approved, he may not have been proud, but he accepted my decisions. I knew I needed help and I was not proud of myself. One cold morning my son was walking to school in the rain, and I felt so bad as a mom without a car. I started thinking about the tax checks I had previously got with nothing to show for it. The drugs were on me bad. I even went to a treatment center on my own because I knew my problem was bad. I only stayed one night and left the next day. I wasn't ready to sober up. I mean I wanted to, but the addiction was stronger than I.

# Turning Point

I got pregnant with my second child during all of this. When I had him, there was a guy who said he was the father. I knew that with all I was doing, it was a possibility it was not his child. He stood strong on the fact that he was his. I kept telling him to get a DNA test, but he refused at first. When my son made 8 months, he got a hold of a cocktail of K-2 (fake marijuana). I was smoking this to help ween myself from the drugs I was using. It was known as "woo" where we're from, which was the strongest fake marijuana available. My son almost died from swallowing some of the drug. He stopped breathing, he turned blue, and I thought I lost him. He was life flighted to Houston Texas, where he was in a coma for 5 days. The guy who stepped up as my son's father entire family was in Houston there to support us. I had never witnessed this type of support in my life. I had to tell the doctor what happened, and I knew CPS was coming for me. I immediately got on a bus to Beaumont to explain to my oldest what was about to happen. I got a ride back to Houston where my son was still in ICU.

When I returned, my son woke up and was healthy as ever, a miracle from God. I remember reading the Bible and praying over my son, something I'd never done before. I told God if He saved him, I won't go back. When my son was saved, that was my crossroads. Either continue in drugs or raise my kids. They were out of my custody for 90 days, the longest 90 days of my life. I found God in this process and held on to Him. He was the only one there to comfort me as I got through that storm. An old drug dealer/friend reached out to me and entertained me on some of those lonely nights. That was when my oldest girl was conceived. I was clean and sober with the power of God on my life. In a way I feel like this guy was sent to turn me back, but with the power of God over my life, I wouldn't. We stopped talking, until a few days before she was born. I then moved to another location, he helped and moved with me. We tried to raise her together. It didn't last for long, then we stopped talking. My daughter was about a year old. I started smoking weed again. Going around others who indulged, while one is trying to put it down will have a person backslide. As I mentioned before, those around you have a funny way of rubbing off on you. That's why it is good to keep yourself separated. This is when you find You, without influences. So, after our thing was over, I met a guy in front of my house. I thought he was heaven sent at first. Then I realized that he was not. He was a good dude, but not stable enough to build. That was why that situation did not last.

Just so happen, the guy who stepped up for my son Jay, (in words) came back into my life through an old friend. His mom provided and cared for my son until she passed. (RIP). I did feel some type of way about him, so I started to chill with him again. I should have known better (it was tax time). I felt foolish and played, but I also knew God was using me. Things were spiraling downhill. My faith was being tested, however my faith in God is what got me through that mess. I was supposed to move to Waco Texas but THANK YOU GOD! I ended up pregnant with my baby girl which prevented me from going to Waco. I finally took a job offer to work at a drug treatment facility with my sister. I was in school when I started the job and was able to move into a nicer house.

It is the Lord's will, that determines what we shall do. I even picked up a few more hours caring for my Ex's grandmother. Everyone faded, my focus is God, my kids, and our future. My prayer is that I will not return to anything God saved me from, that has any rule over my life.

Prayer: Heavenly Father, I ask for discernment in all my affairs. Let me not be influenced by negative entities but help me to be a positive influence. I pray for new relationships for my advancement, also for the strength to help others in their advancement. I need your guidance Lord, show me when to talk and when to be silent. When to move and when to be still.

Amen

# Mom Life

Being a single mother caring for four children, and school for the past three years, while maintaining my household is tough. My oldest is Lavontae (18), he just graduated high school. He has his license, he's very smart and wise. He is a good boy/man. My second is Javion (7), a burst of energy, speaks his mind with no filter, he is one to adore. My third is Lavazia (5), she is so sweet like her Mama, at first. Once you get to know her, she is a force to be reckoned with. My baby girl Lamarya (2), she will be a ray of light and a force to be reckoned with. I have four different fathers for my children, one of which I do not know who he could be. Now, I do not say this proudly, but I do say it unapologetic-ally. I'd rather keep each of my children than to abort them because I messed up.

No, I was not ready to be a parent, especially without the help of the fathers. However, I'll take my babies and try to do the best I can with them. Honestly, (considering my ADHD, it is best to have my hands full with something productive to focus on. Instead of having all this energy and putting it into unproductive things. Everything happens for a reason. I will be great despite of my mistakes or past. The overwhelming spirit it gives can sometimes be a bit much when trying to control my feelings.

But I know God is leading me to the rock that is higher than I, when my heart is overwhelmed. (Psalm 61:2).

I know that He is preparing me for better. The work of my hands is to bring Him glory. He would not give me more than I can bear.

Prayer: Lord, I ask that you give me wisdom and keen discernment in all my affairs. I ask that you keep me steady in all that you have for me to do. Thank you for the strength you have given me and thank you for rest. I asked you send helpers my way so that I would not have to work so hard. Thank you for blessing me to enjoy the fruits of my labor. Help me to be the best mother I can be for my babies and the best role model I can be for all those who look to me (as they look to you). I ask that you bless everyone connected to me and bring peace and joy to them. In Jesus name, Amen

It is a beautiful thing to be able to be there for your seeds without being influenced by the baby father. If I was still with them, I may have been held back in some sort of way. I love them for a reason, but I'm no longer interested in the hobbies they indulge in. Which makes going around them not so comfortable. I saw a post on Facebook about "kids be thinking they have a deadbeat father but the whole time they had a bitter baby Mama." Some women can be identified by this saying, and then there are women like me who would rather the dad not be around, due to the lifestyle they live. True enough every child needs their dad, but what if the dad is strung out on drugs? What if they hung around many different people with no sense of stability? Or if they chose alcohol and to hang in the streets every day? I can't knock what they choose to do in their free time, but I do not have to have my children subjected to things like this. I admit I had my days with all the above, but I now put my children above all those things. I got high in the house and if I wanted to run the streets, I made sure they were somewhere safe. I cannot count on the responsibility of their dad, so I would rather care for my babies myself without putting any pressure on none of their dads. The love I have for my children is indescribable, I love them so much, it hurts at times. Francis Chan said "My desire for my children is only a faint echo of God's great love for us! "The love I have for them and the desire for their love is strong enough to see how much God loves and desires us.

Thinking as a parent, I do overlook some of their shortcomings out of understanding that they are imperfect, just like me. On the other hand, I do get on their behinds more than I would another child because they are my children. So, they will feel my wrath out of love, to set them straight. God does the same thing for His children, by being so merciful but chastening at the same time. The best part of parenting I believe, is seeing how your children interact with one another. It is such a warm feeling to see how they care for and love on one another. Especially right after seeing them have a disagreement. The love between them, will not let a misunderstanding stop them from loving each other. I hope they have a close relationship when they grow up. It will be interesting to see how they interact when they are adults. When I think of me and my siblings, I see that time can tear us apart, but I am learning that the only thing that will keep us apart is pride, unforgiveness, jealousy and envy.

Basically, these things are in a dirty heart and a cluttered mind. Praying to create a clean heart is vital. Renewing the mind with the word is important to ensure the thoughts are directed to fruits of the spirit. If we fill up with the word, we will be emptied of everything that tries to tear us down and destroy our relationships. My sisters are especially important whether they know it or not. We may not talk everyday but the love is there. I pray that our relationships are strengthened spiritually towards one another. Also, that my kids have a strong relationship with one another. Lord be with us, In Jesus name, Amen.

# Walk By Faith

Sometimes it gets lonely when you're walking with God. In a sense of, things you used to want to be around does not fit you anymore. Or people who used to want to be around you, just don't have time for you anymore. This is because God has something, he wants to put in you, something he wants you to see. Sometimes the spirit that is within others can be a hindrance to what God wants to show you. To receive what he has for you, you must be OK with being alone for a season, even a few seasons. Sometimes those around us can be distracting. Especially if they're not trying to build an intimate relationship with God. You wanting to seek him could be irritating to others who may have evil spirits residing in them. They may not want to admit it and you may not see it, but God does.

Trust those moments when you feel like everyone is fading from you, it is for a reason that only God can understand. Further down the road you may see what caused the separation. They say that separation brings elevation. Everyone cannot go where you go, everyone is not chosen to do the same things that He called you to do. People who are in your life for your advancement are not the same as those who are in your life to hold you back. God only see people's true intentions. The world is full of smiling faces. People will smile and joke with you, but not have any good intentions.

If you fall today or tomorrow, they would be glad, but if you were to advance, they would be envious and jealous and will not tell you, or let you see.

Discernment allows one to see what other people are trying to keep to themselves. Everyone around you is not there for your advancement. Many people want you to be stuck in the same habits simply because they have not decided to make a change for themselves. It brings discomfort when you do things for the betterment of yourself. If their mentality is not ready for the shift, your enthusiasm could be poisoned from their wanting to stand still. Separate from these people. Who is meant for you in your level up will gravitate back. When they do, you must figure out if this person who is coming back, is there to support your growth? or bring you back to where you were? Are they looking to you for assistance in their growth or to simply suck you out of your current state? Praying for wisdom and discernment for all who may not know who is good for them and who is not.

Wisdom is on my mind right now. What is wisdom?
According to a definition from Siri, it is the quality of having experience, knowledge, and good judgement, the quality of being wise. To me, it is knowing what to say and when to say it. It is also knowing when to hold your peace. How is wisdom obtained? It is obtained by gaining knowledge in certain areas such as school, church, home, and streets. In my opinion the best and most effective type of wisdom is Godly wisdom, and this can be obtained through prayer and reading the word.

I learned that just because you have a lot of insight does not mean that you must let all your insight known to others. Some things are good to share, but others should be kept to self.

Honestly, this is something that I struggle with. This is wisdom that I still need to mature in. Everyone is not ready to receive a message that you are able to understand at that moment.

Prayer: Lord in Heaven, thank you for everything! I ask that you guide my thoughts to be filled with your wisdom. Give me your wisdom and insight to know when to speak and when to hold my tongue. I confess that I speak on things that I should not sometimes. I ask that you send your holy Spirit to hold my tongue when I may be tempted to speak on things that are not pleasing to you. In Jesus name Amen.

Tears are needed. It can be used as a cleanser to the soul. The pain that one feels is also needed for growth. If life were easy all the time without pain or tears, how would one be able to truly mature into a woman or man? I believe pain teaches us to be humble. Also, there is a time for everything in life. If life were all laughter, many would take it as a joke. If life were all good, one would become prideful. The same as if life were all pain, it would wear one down. Balance is needed to function properly. The reason I say this, is because one cannot go through life without one single emotion and be okay. That would make them a robot in a sense. Feel those different emotions, they each make you stronger and wiser. Always move past the different emotions, never stay stuck feeling one way. Some say, "I am the same all the time." I do not agree with that logic. Could they really react the same if they were angry, sad, happy, stressed, or worried? Maybe my logic is not right, because I have read in a devotional to be the same in every situation. Lord help me to remain at peace regardless of the situation.

I'm thankful for strength to keep going regardless of my condition. When I was an angry person, I did not have good vibes. I reflected what was in me, now with the love of the Lord, I have peace and happiness. Therefore, I seem to others as a nice pushover. However, I am learning to love others with the love of Jesus and have meekness and kindness. Make no mistake, I still have that Lion within me. I will be nice until someone rubs me to the point to where I must show them what is in me. However, I try to keep the peace. "Keep it pushing" is my motto. Satan stand behind me. Now the thoughts are, what if it is all in my head, what if no one is really feeling a type of way. Then............ I realize energies are real, discernment is real, wisdom is real!!

It's a reason a person feels a certain way around others. Either you let it go over your head, or you take heed. Not so much as reacting to it physically but understanding where you stand with those individuals. Bless us with wisdom and discernment. Ephesians 3:16-17 (KJV), That he would grant you according to the riches of his glory, to be strengthened with might by his spirit in the inner man. That Christ may dwell in your hearts by faith: that ye being rooted and grounded in love.

Before having a serious relationship with God, I never felt power, at least not the power I feel when I am in the word. The power away from the word is like a dark power. It is a power that tells you that however you feel is valid, even if it is not fruitful for the right cause.

Through faith, I can feel that righteous power, from hearing the word of God. It is a power that cannot be denied. Listening to the world can take one off course sometimes.

According to 1Corinthians 2:5, Your faith should not stand in the wisdom of men, but in the power of God. Men can only provide you with what they think is best.

However, their thoughts could never reach the depths of God's wisdom. I wish I could say that we would be perfect through the word. If one could be, or if one was, it would cause a sense of pride to come forth. A sense of "I am better because I don't make mistakes", mindset.

Mistakes keep us humble and give us the understanding that we are human. Galatians 5:17-18 (KJV), For the flesh lusteth against the Spirit, and the spirit against the flesh; and these are contrary the one the other; so that ye cannot do the things that ye would. But if ye be led by the spirit, ye are not under the law.

The law is what tells us if an action is not appropriate. However, being led by the spirit is a way to get things going in the realm of highest glory. The human mind cannot comprehend what the Spirit has for us. Proverbs 3:56, trust in the Lord with all thine heart and lean not to your own understanding, in all your ways submit to him and he will make your paths straight.

Sure, I can rely on what I know to get me through, but how far can I go trusting in only my philosophy about life. That is a question that should be asked to countless of successful people, to understand what methods they used to make it through. There are so many beliefs within the human creation. 1Corinthians 12:4-6 KJV states, "now there are diversities of gifts, but the same Spirit. There are differences in administrations, but the same Lord. And there are diversities of operations, but it is the same God which work-eth all in all.

The Lord can use evil forces to make his plan effective. As humans, we wonder why is He considered a good God with everything that happens in the world? The short answer is, it is not fair but a part of the plan. Something to keep in mind is Romans 5:3-5 (KJV)NLT, We can rejoice when we run into problems and into trials, for we know that they help us develop endurance. And endurance develops strength of character, and character strengthens our confident hope of salvation.

Every day is a lesson and a test. Seeking God for guidance shows us how we can understand the lessons and pass the test. We will be tempted, we will fall, we will not do everything perfect or right. However, keep seeking Him, The only thing that will firmly keep you is the word of God. When people think you are losing, (because their mind seems that they are getting over on you) they are the losing one. I like to serve, that's the example Jesus gave. Therefore, I want to resemble it as well. I understand that it is not just about how I feel. It is the love of God that makes me consider others before myself. I honestly think that without my devotion to God I would not have the ability to do what I do. In times past, I would have been in my head about how I feel, what can I get, and forget everything else. But, when the word says it will transform your mind, it is very true! With faith, constantly devoting self to the word, and not trusting in yourself, unlimited amounts of blessings will come and overtake you. Many of which you will not even see happening.

Prayer: Lord, help us to drink from the well that never runs dry, and overflow to everyone around us. In Jesus name, Amen.

Although we might not see ourselves as others see us, we are to speak life to our spirits. We can tear our own spirits down with negative talk and self-doubt. Therefore, the word can help diminish these thoughts. When I rely on my own thoughts, I realize that my plans and my goals are not definite. I can see that it's more than just how I view myself. It is a spirit that God placed inside of me that works as a member to the many others who are a part of God's Kingdom. Sometimes others can see what is on the inside of us that we can't see. These destiny helpers are designed to assist us to reach our purpose. It is when we are down on ourselves with doubt, that destiny helpers can't truly manifest their vision due to the voice telling us to not believe that our purpose is higher than we could ever imagine. Ephesians 3:20 "Now unto him that is able to do exceedingly abundantly above all that we ask or think, according to the power that works in us." Therefore, it is not what we think of ourselves, but rather what the word reminds us about the power that works within us.

# Growth from a worldly perspective to a spiritual perspective

Growth is on my mind. Growth is change. How do things change and grow? From my perspective, growth is something that everyone does, and it is meant for everyone. For instance, babies grow into toddlers, into kids, into teenagers, into adults. They change throughout all these phases, things such as appearance, body, and mind functioning. However, the brain stops growing at the age of 25, many people stay the same form there. Change is something a bit different when we consider growth. Just because a man has grown to be a certain age does not mean he is a changed man.

Change begins by what one feeds the spirit. If it is all worldly indulgences, a man can only grow from a worldly perspective, which will fade. But if he indulges in spiritual exercises, such as reading the Bible with understanding, he will have the ability to surpass what the world wants him to know. That is growth. This is also where change comes, not only in his mind, but overflows to those lives that are connected to his. There are no high-power people, simply, people who are set up in the world with different positions, each being used by God for his purpose. God is the only higher power that exist. The world will try to drain us with so many different beliefs such as all the different religions. It is only when one seeks the truth for themselves, that will help them find the truth that is revealed to them.

It is important to consider what you are and what you believe. A man is as he thinks in his heart Proverbs 23:7. One can drown in their consumption of what they learn. Be careful to ensure that what you learn will provide you with the strength you need to breathe. So, you come back up to life better than you went down. No one that lives this life without a sincere connection to God can grasp the importance of seeking him. It is easy to say, "I put God first", but haven't opened the bible to let God speak. It is only through Him speaking the word of life over them that they can grow and be productive (spiritually). The world will have one thinking it is all about what they can accomplish on earth that matters. The truth is what we do here is something to keep us occupied. Some things have been made as distractions, while other things are made as entertainment. The entertainment keeps us busy doing something, while the distractions are set up to take us off the road we need to be on.

I am learning to overcome evil with good. I could have and keep a stink attitude, or I could adjust and keep those positive vibes flowing, making those negatives ones flee. There is so much more value to life when you put God at the center of it. It brings peace, understanding, hope, joy, love, a caring heart, a powerful mind, and a beautiful spirit.

Relying on one's own strength can be lethal. It is because so many things we think we may know; we really don't have a clue about. Our wisdom is nearly like the trees for a season it last, then it fades away. Next, it flourishes again with new leaves, but it is the same tree. Nothing changes but the seasons that weathers the tree, which God has ordained. "God is that tree, we are the seasons." Every bit of wisdom we possess comes from God. As mentioned in Hosea 4:6, people perish from lack of knowledge. When one tends to lean too much towards their own understanding, they may feel that their worldly wisdom is enough. They should understand that when they pass, every bit of wisdom passes with them. The only wisdom that stays is that of which was taught and learned by others. I believe that those before me believed. The looks of it shows that they may have believed, but not to the extent that would change their ways and views of things. I think that if one is a true believer, they would live like it in the things they do, not just with the things they say.

"They call out to me with their mouths, but their hearts are far from me" (Isaiah 29:13). This is where people get mixed up when watching believers. They see those who say they believe and think, "well how can they believe if their actions do not align with what they say they believe." It is because they just say they believe. Do not misunderstand me, even believers fall short, it is human nature. To tell the difference between true believers and those that speak of being a believer takes discernment and time. Anyone can go to church for a few months, but the faithful few will remain. Even when they are going through the worst time, they do not stop going to God. They stand firm on their beliefs and the fruits they produce shows that God's Spirit dwells within them.

Prayer: Lord, I ask that you send your Spirit so that believers will reign mightily in you. I ask that people will be so in tuned to you that the enemy has no choice but to let your people go! Let your chosen leaders stand boldly so the world can see your light in them and come out of their darkness. Thank you in advance Lord for all that you are about to do. In Jesus name, Amen.

Having thoughts in the mind of people not liking you? Has there been negative energy you have been feeling due to these thoughts? Get off those social sites where you are comparing your life to everyone else. Read a devotion to help correct the thought process. The Lord gave me Romans 8:6; "So letting your sinful nature control your mind leads to death, but letting the spirit control your mind leads to life in peace." This verse came on time for how I was feeling. Sinful nature can be any thoughts that are against the knowledge of God. Thoughts that may have you feeling offended from the opinion of others. Before sin comes it starts in the mind. From reactions to others and not being filled with the word. Negative thought is caused from viewing things not of God.

It is important to stay filled with the word, concerning Matthew 12:43-45 which says, "when an evil spirit leaves the person it goes to the desert seeking rest but finding none. Then it says, "I will return to the person I came from" so it returns and finds its former home empty, swept and in order. Then the spirit finds seven other spirits eviler than himself, and they all enter the person and live there. So, it makes that person worse off than before. That would be the experience of this evil generation. If one is not staying filled, the evil spirit which fled from them comes back stronger. In a sense, I think this is why so many people turned back after they were saved and cleaned, because they forgot to keep seeking Him. With God we can overcome all setbacks. He shows us that time and time again.

With the many things in the world to be involved in, what I think is the most valuable is being able to pour into others. You could have a lot and, know a lot, but what good is it if you keep it all to self, is it really a lot? There are many people in the world to share some of what you have with. Sometimes things such as fear, and anxiety prevents one from reaching out to others. Fear of what others may think and anxiety of what could go wrong. These are my main struggles with sharing with others. I am coming to terms that this way of thinking is only crippling my destiny. Being fearless is how to let the light shine.

Prayer: Lord I ask that you give me a fearless and bold spirit. Keep me humble and compassionate. Help me to be stern and genuine with all my encounters. Keep my eyes on you in all that I do. In Jesus name, Amen.

I have not accomplished anything huge yet, I plan to in the future. I will do great things in God; this is my declaration! I will leave a legacy for my great grandchildren; they will know who I am. Generational curses are broken in the name of Jesus. I will have all that our Father in Heaven has for me.

# Opinions are everywhere, so is Truth

Every opinion that is given is merely a perspective from a point of view. Everyone doesn't hold the same values; therefore, everyone is not conditioned to like or approve the same things. It is so much easier to stand on how we feel about a certain issue than to take others views and consider them. Sure, I know what I know, but what can I gain from other perspectives? It is something that I was blind to, or just a lesson I skipped while maturing. These are questions that I am starting to consider. I do not want to be tossed like the winds, to and fro, falling for everything everyone has to say. But, if there is anything at all that I can apply to my life that would make me a better person, I would gladly make it my takeaway. However, to be willing to listen to someone you must have an open mind. Thinking your way is the only way, can blind you to the possibilities that could assist your growth. Things that you may have learned already, but just need some refreshment.

Prayer: Lord, help us to be open in all that we come across. Bless us with new relationships while directing us, as we receive direction from constructive criticism. Let us take these things and learn from them and not have a wall that prevents us from humbling ourselves by learning something new. In Jesus name, Amen.

Opinions, there are so many of them. They go hand in hand with values, morals, beliefs, and backgrounds. The question is, does anybody's opinion matter? I can say how I feel about a certain situation all day long but does the way I feel about it even matter? One day when I leave this body, every opinion I ever thought of will no longer exist. It would just be about the way other people feel about certain things. Then, they will die off too. What is a lasting foundation that will stand forever? My guess is Truth, God's Truth. There are two things certain in life and that is good and evil. Evil is, in my mind a force that tries to pull everyone down from their True purpose. Evil (the devil) comes to kill, steal, and destroy. Good, in my mind, is something that everyone has deep down. It just depends on what they feed to make larger, the good or the evil. There is a saying that mentions, "apples don't fall too far from the tree." I think of this in a sense that you are what you come from. Let's say that my parents were good in some form but evil in others. Both traits may pass down, however, it is more of what I indulge in that will stick.

Yes, there will be genes that I have from them, but the mindset is a powerful field that can take over what is truly inside. Same thing with good parents with children who are not so good. It's all in the mind of those who overcome what is within them. In the Bible it states that, "Faith comes by hearing the word of God. Romans 10:17 If this is true, ill intentions may come from hearing evilness from other sources. We are not only made of what was inherited, but we are what we know. If we only knew destruction, that is what we will contribute. If we only know peace and love, it is easier to give.

From experience, I used to be what my mom called a "demon child." I would raise all types of hell. I stayed angry and I wanted to fight all the time. I would get mad at the drop of a dime, and nobody could tell me nothing, because I was on a rampage. Once I got in my word and saw myself in some of the verses, (proverbs taught me a lot about me). I was like whoa I didn't want to be that person anymore. I started to see myself in a new light with constantly reading the Bible. It is like it cleansed me from the filth that I was drenched in. Don't get me wrong, I'm still human, but me staying in my word helps me get a reality check when I'm not right.

How many times can one fall? Every day comes with lessons that were not evident the day before. Some days we know when temptation tries to take hold of us. Other days, those tempting situations are dressed as opportunities for fun, (flesh fun). However, in those moments where we fall, we should cry out to God and ask him to deliver us. Not only from the world, but from ourselves. We can be our own worst enemy and not even be aware of it. "Create in us a clean heart and renew a righteous spirit within us." Psalms 51:10.

One of my favorite verses is, "My flesh and my heart may fail, but God is the strength of my heart and my portion forever Psalm 73:26. I love this verse because I am sure to fall, but I know that God is my strength. So, to answer the first question "how many times one can fall?" Proverbs 24:16 says, "For a just man falleth seven times and rises again, but the wicked shall fall into mischief. If we are righteous, we will rise. Seven times in my perspective, means at least once a day. Henceforth, standing strong in the Lord gives us the grace to rise again.

Why is it so hard to just stay on the right road, to do everything right? How can a person be all that everyone wants them to be? For one, it is evident that all men turn aside and not one is good, Romans 3:12 says, "all has turned away, they have altogether become useless. No one does good, not even one. That is the reason why it is so hard to stay on the right road every moment of life. Trying to be who others want us to be is exhausting. If we work too hard, they tell you to take a break. If you have too much time on your hands, they tell you to work. There is no way we can please everyone around us. Sometimes they see things in us, that we don't see in ourselves. However, they can't force us to change. Therefore, we are only responsible for what we choose to implement in our lives from others. We are everything that God calls us to be. The one each human should strive to be like, is Christ. Everyone else are simply walking imperfections.

Each new day brings lessons and battles. It is important to guard the mind with the shield from the word to win the battles and enjoy the blessings. Only going off our own strength, the battles that rage around us can get inside of us and leave our spirit beat down, while our hopelessness blinds us to the blessings. The word helps us to acknowledge that even through the trials and the errors, he will not leave us. It is trusting him through it all that helps us overcome these moments when we feel we can't go on. While the battle is the Lord's, we are to embrace the blessings and let the Lord fight the battle using what he has instilled in us. Sometimes it's not comfortable, but in those moments of pressure, rest assured he is molding you into a diamond.

Prayer: Dear Lord, help us to always look to you when we go through the battles. Overwhelm us with your love and comfort us in these moments. Help us to feel your presence and have your way in our lives. Thank you in advance for lovingly overwhelming us with your love and spirit, In Jesus name Amen.

# Love Covers All

All the world need is good love. I think hate was created so that it could give people an option to choose from, the choice of freedom. Either love or hate is what people carry in their hearts, I look at hate as a blinder. When one is filled with hate, they cannot see the good in anything. Instead, it pours out of their mouth, into the atmosphere, trying to damage anything it could. On the other hand, love is a light, it shines brightly while trying to mend everything in his path. Although, it is a hard love, it covers everything. Love is needed to make individuals thrive. Imagine how children who have not been shown love may feel in this world, how empty and lonely they may feel? The ones that are not filled with love end up being cold- hearted individuals. Sometimes violent and other times depressed. As stated in the Bible, this world is ruled by the prince of darkness (John 12: 31). So, if he can darken the eyes of the people, he can fill their minds with hate and close their minds to the truth of matter. Love covers a multitude of sins, and a loving heart is a healthy heart.

Being a nice person can incline others to believe that you are a pushover, gullible, naive person. I feel that there is a thin line between being nice and being taken advantage of. People who think of themselves as a high rank in the world, mentally or financially have their way of taking those who would do anything for them and making them out to be a "fool" because they feel they can get away with it. However, there is no way of getting away with, using, or rather being an enemy to God's children. God has his way of repaying us for our deeds whether good or bad. If we look at the model Jesus shows, we could see that he was meek and lowly, but he didn't play the fool. He was compassionate with all that crossed his path, but he didn't let what the Pharisees or even the tempts from the devil make him step out of character or do anything that was against the word of God.

My prayer today is, Father in heaven help us to not let this world or the things in it tempt us. Give us a meek gentle spirit that shows your character, because ours is not always pleasing to you. Help to build our character like Jesus and all we say and do. Let us not back down when you want us to stand. In Jesus name, Amen.

A kind person would get more respect than an evil person. Kindness will take you far if you use it in the right ways towards all men. Sometimes it's hard to be kind to a person who's mean to you. Personally, I do feel they may take it as they got a one up on you if you fail to respond. But the reality of it is, you don't have to entertain nothing you don't want to, that includes the ignorance of others and their attitudes. Let them think what they want to think. At the end of the day, they are building their karma, you are exchanging energy with them (or not) is building yours.

No matter how tough you see others act, they know someone can do them in. Many just want to feel better because their self-esteem is not where it should be. A person with high self-esteem does not inflict pain on others. Neither do they treat others bad to feel better, they understand that kindness and respect is the way to go. Prayer: Lord, I ask that you send your spirit down so that we can have more laborers for your work. People with integrity, kindness and respect for self and others.

Let the spirit rub off on all you assigned to it. In Jesus name, Amen.

The key to dealing with smiling faces is keeping a guard on your heart and never trusting men. Only through trusting God you can see to the schemes of people. The spirit of discernment can bless your natural sight in many ways. With business matters it could feel that you weren't going anywhere, and your coworkers do not like you, making you drained to the point you stop putting your best foot forward. Pause to pray, Father in heaven, we ask you to strengthen us when the world tries to drain us, let your spirit pour out upon us, so we can reach our highest purpose you have for us. In Jesus name, Amen.

The church can be a place many turn from due to only seeing the natural state of those within. Some don't seem to grasp the fact that everyone has something they do that makes them human. The people in the church are trying to make it, they know that they are sick and need healing. The thing is when we tend to point out the mistakes of others, forgetting that we have fallen short too, it makes those without much spiritual understanding feel unworthy.

Everyone has something they are afraid to share with others out of fear of how they will view them, or how they would be accepted once known. I guess that is the best part of being in a relationship with God, He knows everything concerning you, yet he still loves you the same. He understands our nature better than we do. Sometimes we can be so caught up with what we have on our minds, we forget to consider our ways are not his ways, neither are our thoughts His. Instead, we tend to lean on our understanding. However, what if our truth could be a light to another? What if more of us shared our truths without the fear of what others may think?

Pause to pray: Father God in Heaven, help us to express our true selves boldly without doubt, shame, or apologies. Lord help us to walk as you intended for us to walk without fear, but with power, love, and a sound mind. Thank you in advance Lord! Let us walk with full confidence, knowing that God is using us for His glory. Let your glory shine through us Lord. In Jesus name, Amen.

The Lord wants to live through us. He blesses us, so that we can be a blessing to others. Deeds done in vain have fruitless outcomes. Vanity is doing things our own way. The spirit of the Lord dwells in all who consistently seek him. The word is power! The pandemic we faced was a way of getting our attention. The church was never about a building. It was about renewing the mind, cleaning the heart and letting His glory shine through all that we do. Sad to say, the only communion many people have with God is on Sundays. Even then, their minds and hearts are not completely surrendered. They worry about their looks, others look, what that person did, and why is this person acting like this? The focus was off in many buildings. With the churches closed for the Pandemic the atmosphere was being shifted, so God can live through us. He wants all hearts inclined to him without distraction. Once He gets inside our hearts fully, as His will desire, we can then be a blessing to others. However, relying on God is the only way to have fruitful outcomes. Hallelujah!

## My experiences with Mental Health

My experience with mental illness involves depression, anxiety disorder, bipolar disorder, addictive behaviors, and ADHD. Wow, reading that I am really messed up, That is only in my strength, but God's presence can transform any situation. When my dad left, I faced depression, I was sad, agitated at the world, and felt hopeless. This lowered my self-esteem in so many ways. If you knew the bond I had with my dad, you would understand why this affected me so much. I was about eleven years old when I started to experience the side effects of anxiety. My mind would be everywhere. I couldn't keep my thoughts focused on one thing. I would have no Peace of Mind with anxiety. Another mental illness that I went through was bipolar disorder which causes mood swings. I would be happy at one second, sad the next, and angry the next, and this is all in a 20-minute period. I had no control over it. Still working to live with it better.

By the time I turned seventeen, I knew my addictive behaviors were a problem. My mind was not stable enough to get far. I was living in darkness; I would go whichever way the wind blew because of my low self-esteem and lack of guidance. ADHD is another mental illness that I have, that I wasn't aware how it affected me until I was in my 20's. I would wonder why I couldn't focus and why I have all the extra energy. Once I identified it, I was able to see that it was difficult to be around one with ADHD, but also, it's a gift to be able to have energy to get things done. When the mind is idle, the devil can really play with thoughts. Therefore, when dealing with mental illness, it is so important to stay under the word of God. The devil can't mess with your head as much if you transform it with the word daily. The only thing that gives the Satan power over the mind is the choice of not seeking God.

## **Mental Illness Background:**

Mental health is a condition of well-being where a person acknowledges their own potential, being able to give back to their community, manages the normal stresses of life, and work adequately. Depression, anxiety disorders, schizophrenia, eating disorders and addictive behaviors are all examples of mental illness. It is written "that young adult who prayed daily tend to have fewer depressive symptoms, and high levels of life satisfaction, self-esteem, and positive affect, in comparison to those who never prayed."

Life has a way of taking individuals with mental illnesses and making them believe that they are not worth much due to their mental capability. This is a lie of the enemy. When we posture self with God's purpose for our life, we can see how worthy we truly are. A relationship with the higher power introduces one to abilities, capacities, and aptitudes they did not know they had. There is no cure for mental illness. However, having a connection with the higher self, or higher power will help them to maintain their condition. Although, research has been done to see the effects of spirituality on mental wellness. There is still more to be found about why not everyone receives wellness as they practice spiritual formation. Religion has been shown to have both positive and negative influence on the individual life of human beings. The goal is to explore the thoughts of one being eased of their mental illness by becoming in deep touch with the spiritual aspect of life. To effectively obtain a clearer mind with mental illness one can exercise spiritual activities, pray with faith consistently for deliverance, and do the work to heal from traumas.

**<u>Spiritual Struggle</u>:**

Some individuals feel that God is not real, because if he were, why would he allow humans to be flawed and suffer? This causes spiritual struggle among many people. Many have been blinded, wanting to do things their way.

According to John 12:40 "He has blinded their eyes and hardened their hearts, they do not see with their eyes nor understand with their hearts, nor turn- and have me heal them." Also, God will give us up to our desires as well.

Romans 1:24 "God gave them over in the lusts of their hearts to impurity, so that their bodies would be dishonored among them."

The limitation for the power within the word is everyone does not have access to the word in certain locations. The limitations that were found may have impacts on the outlook considering the misconceptions and desirability of receiving the word. Especially the correcting part of the word where pride blocks healing. I can structure my outlook to reduce limitation by acknowledging that everyone will not believe, it's the chosen ones he is calling. When we understand that everything is not for everyone, we could see this is where the limitations will stand. When one is blinded and the heart hardened from the pains of life, leaves them limited in their capabilities.

## Most Recent Events

In the last house in Beaumont, I felt it was time for me and my kids. My oldest sister moved out of town, and I thought that it was a great idea to move where I had some sort of family support. I found a house after a few trips back and forth. I really couldn't afford that house, and at the time I was not working. I am thankful that house did not go through. I probably would have had more problems maintaining it as opposed to living in an apartment. The price ranges are a little more expensive this way. I ended up finding an apartment (the first apartment in 10 years), however it was where I needed to be. I met a neighbor who gave me the scoop on everything. I could talk to her, and she gave me the words I needed. According to Proverbs 18:24, a man of many companions may come to ruin but there is a neighbor who sticks closer than a brother. I don't have many people I associate with, but it nice to have a friend. God placed me where there's help to get my kids on the bus, a lunch lady who provided lunch after school, and I was able to get a caretaker to get them off the bus and start their homework. You can be scared to make a change from the norm, but when God is in it, there is no limit. Trust him. Again, I say His plan is way better than our plans in life. I was able to find a work from home position. Now for the first time in my life, I am not eligible for food stamps or housing. I am confident that God is parting the seas in my life. It all starts with renewing our minds and trusting in God's plan.
Knowing that in Him we find our purpose, joy and strength.

I have a special seasoning blend as well, although anyone can make their own. However, what makes it special is the love I put in it. "Lesley's Love" is the name of my seasonings. When we cook or prepare with love everything is better. My goal is to have them on the shelves in stores. God willing.

I also aspire to be a life coach with Love Living Life Coach Ministries.

## The Devil is a Liar

There are individuals who break you to make themselves. They must feel proud when they have taken something from others, leaving them in a messed-up situation. These individuals are doing the enemy's work. There are countless scams going, and they really think they are winning. The reality of the matter is, they are creating their Karma, and just when they want to get right; they will face it. Upon me completion of this book, a situation arose to where I was left with almost nothing after completely paying the publication of this book. You would think when you enter an agreement; if you do your part, the other party will do theirs. This is not the case for those things that were designed to break you. Fighting back can only hinder my peace. I was placed in a position where I stopped writing, felt left out, not guided and I had no more in me. I had to get my power back!

Proverbs 16:9- we can make our plans, but the Lord determines our steps. I could have given up, but I worked too hard. I looked at it as an opportunity to get my branding done. I had faith in this person, but it was a prime example of why to trust God only. God will place the right people in your life who will help you reach the destination he has for us. I am grateful for my new Publisher who was sent from God.

I was reflecting on why I could never connect with many others. It was revealed to me that God places us in a place where our spirits are sensitive to what is around, and he does not want me to be in the mix with too many people's energy that does not align with mine. God wants us to be able to hear him. Love others, but highlight the closest relationships, and make sure that God is at the top of the list. Keep getting up and showing up is what I tell myself and You in this moment. Use those situations that are designed to knock you down as fuel to the fire within. We all break, but Those who wait on the Lord shall find new strength, Isaiah-40:31.

Find your strength and purpose in God. Let no man define you, only by God's spirit and word can we be defined.

I no longer wonder why me? It is evident why now, to let God's will be done.

**Closing Prayer:**

Father in Heaven, thank you for all that you are doing in our lives! I ask that you forgive us for all our sins known and unknown, help us to be all that you have called us to be. Help us to overcome the chains of the enemy that tells us we are nothing. Help us to love like you love us. Lord bless our families, our children, our hopes and dreams. I ask that you Send your spirit to restore and revive your people's lives. Bless the readers to have a different mindset upon completion of this book and I ask that you have your way Lord. Thank you for all that you are doing for us Lord! In Jesus name, Amen.

# Authors Bio

Lesley Lofton, a 33 yr. old single mother of four children. One on the way to college, two in elementary school, and one who was recently potty trained.

Lesley once lived the street life with no regard to bettering herself. It was the environment she grew up in, and the choices she made that led to the spiral of self-destructive behaviors. Lesley struggled with coping with life and began to experience anxiety and depression, which caused her to use drugs as a way of dealing with her mental disorders. Lesley battled with her addiction for some time and drastically changed her life after almost losing her youngest son due to her drug addiction. It was the beginning of her journey.

Lesley used the word of God to gain an understanding of the hand she was dealt. She began to hold herself accountable and take personal responsibility for, not only who she was, but also who she is destined to be for her children. Lesley says, "Her children will experience a better life and she will see to that! God willing."

Lesley has been strong in the word of God for the past five years and uses the word to triumph over her addiction and behaviors. Her sobriety date is December 4, 2015.

Lesley received her Bachelor of Science in Psychology and is a certified Master Life Coach. Hobbies include cooking, devotionals and taking care of home.

www.ingramcontent.com/pod-product-compliance
Lightning Source LLC
LaVergne TN
LVHW051210080426
835512LV00019B/3192